G000155836

A BOOT UP

NORTH WILTSHIRE PUBS

Robert Wood

First published in Great Britain in 2014
Copyright text and photographs
© 2014 Robert Wood

All rights reserved. No part of this publication
may be reproduced, stored in a retrieval system,
or transmitted in any form or by any means without
the prior permission of the copyright holder.

British Library Cataloguing-in-Publication Data
A CIP record for this title is available from the
British Library

ISBN 978 0 85710 088 7

PiXZ Books
Halsgrove House, Ryelands Business Park,
Bagley Road, Wellington, Somerset TA21 9PZ
Tel: 01823 653777
Fax: 01823 216796
email: sales@halsgrove.com

An imprint of Halstar Ltd, part of the
Halsgrove group of companies
Information on all Halsgrove titles is available at:
www.halsgrove.com

Printed and bound in China by
Toppan Leefung Printing Ltd

Contents

How to use this book

The Area

The watery vein that runs through North Wiltshire is not the Thames, which soon disappears into Oxfordshire, but the Kennet & Avon canal. It features in three of the walks and could be said to constitute the southern boundary of North Wiltshire, at least for the purposes of these walks. Only the Wexcombe walk lies south of the waterway. Canal walking has its own charm and I hope I have not overdone it.

Throughout the area there is a pleasing mix of downland (the Marlborough Downs and the downs above the M4 east of Swindon) and woods and forest (West Woods and Savernake Forest). The ridges can be mentioned too. They offer opportunities to secure unforgettable views of the countryside around. A good example is the Bincknoll Castle walk with its superb views north to Swindon. Bincknoll lies on a ridge that runs southwestwards from south-east of Swindon to north-east of Calne. South-west of Marlborough is the ridge occupied by the Wansdyke Way (featured in the Wansdyke and West Woods walk); also the Tan Hill Way further west.

As might be expected, the Romans were here and feature in four of the walks. It was when forging a route from Winchester to Cirencester that they arrived at an obstacle they were obliged most unusually to circumvent (see the Wexcombe walk).

The Civil War was here too, in Malmesbury, on the Aldbourne walk where there was a tussle in 1643, and north of Devizes at Roundway Hill where the Royalists won their last victory later in 1643.

Having surveyed the area once again in order to write these notes I am obliged to assert that with its variety there can be fewer better areas for walking. And the pubs aren't bad either.

The Routes

All the walks are circular. They vary from 3½ miles (but just the one) up to 9 miles and are graded from one to two boots — from easy to fair to more challenging although as it turns out there are no three boot walks in this book although perhaps one or two come close. Routes follow public rights of way or occasionally unmarked but sanctioned tracks, or across open access land. Please remember that conditions under foot will vary greatly according to the season and the weather. Other than that all seasons have something going for them depending on taste; readers will have their own preferences. Weather-wise the best day I had was the Wexcombe walk which I did on the last day of January. This book is no different from others in assuming that the great majority of walkers will arrive by car.

The countryside is never free of danger but the greatest risk comes when crossing roads or walking alongside them or crossing a railway track — rare, but one instance here.

Concerning the Pubs

It is quite possible that the menus you find will vary from what I have said. Or that the management has changed. That happens in which case the menus have more than likely changed. Those things are beyond my control. In these circumstances I have tried my best in the space available to me to convey the spirit and ambience of the establishments featured here.

The Maps

A map is needed to locate the starts and to check out the routes. The sketch maps can only be a rough guide. Six OS maps are needed — Explorer 157 (mostly), 130,131,156, 168 and 169.

In Conclusion

I hope you enjoy the walks and the pubs as much as I did. Wiltshire being such a large county the size dictates two books, so look out for South Wiltshire next. My thanks to Andrew Smith for his shot of Bincknoll Castle; also to Kevin Farmer for his shot of the site of the long deserted settlement of Shaw, and to Gillie Rhodes for her atmospheric picture of the meeting of the ways on the edge of Gopher Wood. All usage complies with the Geograph Creative Commons Licence.

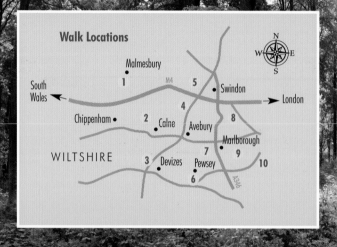

Walk Locations

Malmesbury

1

M4

5

Swindon

→ London

South Wales ←

4

8

Chippenham •

2

Calne

Avebury

+ •

Marlborough

WILTSHIRE

3

Devizes

7

9

Pewsey

10

6

A346

N
W E
S

Key to Symbols Used

Level of difficulty:

Easy

Fair

Map symbols:

Park & start

••••• Walk route

Road

Canal/water

Railway line

■ Building

+ Church

▲ Landmark

 Pub

1 Malmesbury and Little Somerford

No walk with Malmesbury at its heart can disappoint but there is much else here to commend it, not least the gentle river views.

The jewel of this walk is Malmesbury, an enduring medieval treasure. The route

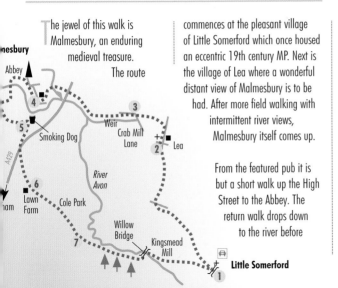

commences at the pleasant village of Little Somerford which once housed an eccentric 19th century MP. Next is the village of Lea where a wonderful distant view of Malmesbury is to be had. After more field walking with intermittent river views, Malmesbury itself comes up.

From the featured pub it is but a short walk up the High Street to the Abbey. The return walk drops down to the river before

Level: 🥾

Length: 7 miles

Terrain: Not too taxing, a few stiles.

Park and Start: St James, Little Somerford (GR 966843). St James is to the left or right from the centre of the village depending on the direction you come in on.

Map: OS Explorer 168

crossing fields to eventually skirt the fine mansion of Cole Park and reach the River Avon where it passes Kingsmead Mill, the home at different times of an inventor and a film producer.

1 Staying on the same side of the road as the church walk away from the village for 100 yards or so. To the right by the curve in the road is a pair of footpath signs, one to Kingsmead and one to Lea. Take the one to Lea. Go through a series of gates, open and shut, all the while veering to the left as you climb up through the fields. Once a road is spotted walk parallel to it towards some farm buildings on the other side of the road. Go past the farm and at the left end of the field pass through a gate and head downhill, keeping over to the right and crossing three stiles as you go. After the last stile shoot down a narrow passage to reach the village of Lea.

2 Cross over the road and pass the church and the pub. To the left is Rushcroft Close. As you make your way to the far right corner be prepared for a glorious view of Malmesbury. Cross the stile and veer right at 45 degrees towards a gate. Head left down a clearly marked track towards a stile at the bottom of the field. Proceed towards the river but

Malmesbury skyline

just before reaching it turn left and walk a few yards before turning right to cross two stiles and reach Crab Mill Lane.

3 Just past the house is a gate to the right with an arrow marked on it. Cross the old bridge over the weir to reach a stile and then another. Keep left and head for a gap in the hedge. Follow the river in an open space where once a railway passed through until it becomes

The Smoking Dog

necessary to hop up the bank and negotiate a gated feature. Now continue along the line of the disused line towards Malmesbury. With the Bowls Club to the right continue past St John's Street to emerge very shortly into the High Street. Turn right uphill to arrive almost immediately at the Smoking Dog.

The Smoking Dog. The dog puffing away impassively on a clay pipe could be Gromit. For starters there will be home-made seasonal soups, such as parsnip, and a collation of cold meats; also filled breads and a variety of burgers. The main course might be beer-battered haddock or a home-made pie of the day. The regular ale is Brain's Reverend James but there will be others. Opening hours for lunch are 12 to 3; telephone 01666 825823.

View back up to the Abbey

(4) Walk up the High Street to the Abbey.

Malmesbury contains so much to see and to imagine. In the Civil War it was said to have changed hands as many as seven times and although it was for Parliament the town had to feed and house soldiers of both sides for much of the war. Although ruined, the Abbey is still the centre-piece of the town. It has seen some sights. In 1010 Brother Eilmer attempted to emulate what jackdaws do but only crashed ignominiously into a meadow. There is a stained glass window in the Abbey showing a monk holding a pair of bat-like artificial wings.

When you are ready to leave the Abbey precincts take Birdcage Walk which is down to the left. At a road go left and then, as the road bends, go right. Follow the path past a private development and cross the right-angled bridge to the other side of the Avon. Somewhere around here, in what one writer called a 'damp thicket', is Daniel's Well.

Tough hombres you have to say, these Malmesbury clerics – or just plain daft. Bishop Daniel, it is said, would spend the night up to his neck in the icy water of the well praying hard to "reduce the force of his rebellious body". No comment.

Moving away from the town follow the river until a path comes in from the right. Take that path and walk uphill towards an old piece of farm furniture. Immediately after passing through a gate go left and proceed up to a stile at the next field boundary. Carry on downhill towards a farm lane that is visible ahead. By the lane and in a corner is a stile. Walk up the lane to reach a main road – the

A429 – where a hospital can be seen opposite.

(5) Cross over the road and turn right, using the pavement. You are looking for a track off to the left which comes up after a few hundred yards. The best way to spot it is to cross to the other pavement and look across until you see the track beside a house. In the distance is Lawn Farm. Aim for a point to the left of the farm, away from the bulk of the complex. There you will find a permissive path that skirts the farm.

(6) As the farm lane curves right, look hard for a signed path on the left that will take you into a large field. The path you want may not be visible but you need to aim for

Cole Park

the right of a large tree. Once past this tree look for a stile on the field edge. On the other side is the Cole Park estate. Follow the line of the fence to arrive at the driveway leading to the house.

Cole Park is the home of Anouska Hempel, the actress – she appeared in the 1969 Bond vehicle 'On Her Majesty's Secret Service' with one-shot George Lazenby as Bond. Later she developed careers as hotelier and designer.

Cross the drive and go straight over another electric fence using the piping. With the house on your left carry on until you come to another electric fence. Notice the moat on your left. Make sure to keep it on your left. Now walk over the hill ahead and down to a gate at the bottom.

(7) Proceed across a short field and then fork left towards the river. Aim for the end of the hedge and once there make a dink to the right to enter an open space beside the River Avon. Ahead you will see a narrow corridor between the river to your left and Angrove Wood to your right. Once through the corridor head for a gate that will be visible ahead. Pass through the gate and continue to a bridge — Willow Bridge. Over to the

Willow Bridge

right, a little way along Mill Lane, is Kingsmead Mill.

Not so long ago Kingsmead Mill was the home of the inventor James Dyson ("I liked the fact that it was once an industrial building"), and before him the film producer David Puttnam.

Where Mill Lane turns to the right and there is a house to the left cross over into an open space. At the far right

corner of the space is the fork you encountered at the start.

Little Somerford had a pub until recently. It was called the Saladin Inn. Why was it named after the dread adversary of Richard the Lionheart? Walter Powell, MP for Malmesbury, moved to Little Somerford in 1878. He was a keen hot air balloonist but while out in 1881 he lost control and was last seen heading across the Channel in his beloved balloon, the Saladin.

There is a lane before the church. Walter Powell's home was down there. The church is worth a stop for the medieval wall paintings.

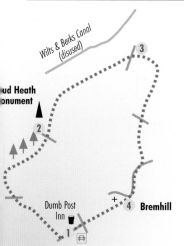

2 Bremhill and Maud Heath

The stellar attraction of this little ramble is the unique Maud Heath monument. Add the stunning views in all directions, a pub with a talking point, a very pretty village, and there is nothing to disappoint.

The queen of this walk is Maud Heath, a widow who in 1474 bequeathed a sum of money to build and maintain a causeway from Wick Hill to Chippenham across flood-prone country so there would be a dry (or drier) pathway for country folk to walk to and from market. Starting at an old country inn with an interesting pedigree the route heads to Wick Hill and the Maud Heath Monument. After a look from a distance at the disused Wilts and Berks canal the route drops down to Bremhill, a quintessential English rural village,

Level: 🥾
Length: 3½ miles
Terrain: One steep descent, one slight climb.
Park and Start: The Dumb Post Inn, close to Bremhill, itself easily reached from Chippenham or Calne (GR 975728).
Map: OS Explorer 156

before arriving back at the pub. After completing the walk why not drive the few miles to the spot where Maud's causeway really mattered? At a little place called Kellaways there is a sequence of 64 raised arches.

There appears to have been a hostelry on the site of the Dumb Post Inn since the 1660s, the establishment being on the old coach route from Bath to Calne. Concerning the name it seems that locals would habitually use holes in the post to leave messages. It is still the practice to stick announcements on the present post. For sustenance expect dishes like pie with fresh peas and homemade quiche along with sandwiches, toasted or not, and filled rolls. On Sundays there are roasts. At the bar the ales are rotated, with 6X a fixture. Eating outside is a definite option. Note that the establishment is not open for lunch on Mondays, Tuesdays and Wednesdays. Otherwise lunch is served from 12 to 2.30 but best in any case to check opening hours on 01249 813192.

The Dumb Post Inn

1. After leaving the pub take the road to the left sign-posted to Studley which at once descends steeply. At the bottom of the incline, and just before a house, go right over a stile and then up a field past a spring before crossing another stile. Go up through some woods to reach a road. Cross over it and go through a gate. At the end of the field where another track crosses, turn right and continue

Maud Heath Monument

along this track until a minor road is reached.

2 You are almost at the Maud Heath Monument, erected in 1838. On the wall to the left is a stone which records the local vicar's

FROM THIS WICK-HILL
BEGINS THE PRAISE
OF MAUD HEATH'S GIFT
TO THESE HIGHWAYS

THE TRANSLATION INTO ENGLISH
VERSE OF THE EARLIER LATIN
INSCRIPTION ON THIS STONE WAS
MADE BY THE REV. W.L. BOWLES
VICAR OF BREMHILL IN 1837

Maud Heath stone

translation of the original Latin tribute to Maud. The inscription he came up with was not however universally admired. This is the point where Maud Heath's Causeway starts. Now cross the road and prepare yourself for a treat. There it is – the monument! What a knockout it is.

Maud sits aloft with her basket, gazing towards Chippenham until the end of time. As for the basket it surely can be read as a sign of solidarity with the people she so much wanted to help.

When you have had your fill of this marvellous and most unusual of obelisks, continue in the same direction as before. When a five-way junction of tracks appears go straight across and follow the contour up to a road and a gate. Down below at the first line of trees was once a working canal – the Wilts & Berks Canal.

The Wilts & Berks Canal ran from the Thames at Abingdon (when it was in Berkshire) to the Kennet & Avon Canal near Melksham. Abandoned in 1914, it may just be on the way to a comeback. Stretches are being restored but not as yet this stretch.

Over to the left on the far ridge can be seen the Lansdowne Monument at Cherhill, erected in 1845 by the same aristocrat responsible for the Maud Heath Monument and, with its elegant tapering, looking like a classy salt cellar. The monument is reckoned to be the highest point between London and Bristol.

3 Cross over and enter a field. At the other side of the field is a stile. Once over it turn immediately right to follow the hedge line.

After a while cross a minor road (Turf House Lane) and then, on joining another minor road, turn right and walk into Bremhill. Formerly also

Bremhill Cross

known as "Brimble", Bremhill is a very a pleasant corner of the world with its stepped cross (restored), its church and its old houses all in close proximity.

4 Go up to St Martin's church (c1200) and pick out a path that skirts the churchyard. Pass through an old iron gate and continue to another old iron gate on the right. Proceed past the fine Manor House to reach a road and the Dumb Post Inn.

Once you are ready to depart the immediate vicinity do make that short drive to Kellaways and the 64 arches (946757) where Maud Heath took on and conquered the Avon marshes.

Bremhill House

3 Devizes and Roundway Hill

Starting in Devizes the walk spreads its wings to take in a section of the Kennet & Avon Canal, a stretch of the old London to Bath road (plenty of scope there for the imagination), and the site of a Civil War battle in 1643.

The canal is not joined immediately; instead a side trip is made to the Crammer, a stretch of water in the heart of Devizes that is strongly associated with the tale of the Moonrakers. On the canal itself there is an insight into canalside living before the route leaves the canal and heads north to the village of Bishops Cannings for a handy pub stop. The remains of the old London to

Level: 🥾 🥾
Length: 8½ miles
Terrain: Canal walking offers no fears. There are two slightly uphill stretches.
Park and Start: Roundway Park, Devizes at the point where it is crossed by the Wessex Ridgeway (GR 011626).
Map: OS Explorer 157

Bath road – the Great Road – come next and soon afterwards Roundway Hill, scene of the Royalists' last success in the Civil War.

19

1 Perhaps it is the name but Quakers' Walk is so tranquil, the perfect way to begin a walk especially as it soon links up with the Kennet & Avon Canal, serene as only canals can be. Cross the bridge and head into the centre of Devizes. Over to the left is a handsome church with its high tower. The fine lake is called the Crammer, home to ducks, geese

Quaker's Walk

and swans, and associated with a peculiarly Wiltshire legend. Cue the Moonrakers.

To join the canal follow the main road past the church curving left as you go. At the canal bridge turn right and go down a slope to gain the towpath.

2 As you go, take in the stylish residences on the opposite side of the canal. At Horton Bridge — the third bridge — it is time to leave the canal. Go under the bridge and

Two Wiltshiremen, engaged in smuggling brandy, hid a barrel of the contraband from the excisemen in a pond. When they returned at some later time, in the dark, they were caught in the act of raking the barrel back to land. Thinking quickly, the smugglers played dumb: "Arrr - we be raking for that girt big cheese". Seeing that the smugglers were looking at the reflection of the full moon, the revenue men burst out laughing at these thick-as-two-short-planks yokels, and left the villagers to their "cheese". By the way, 'Moonraker' applies to all Wiltshire folk.

The Crammer

Des res on the canal

then immediately double back up an incline.

3 Once through the gate turn right on the road and more or less instantly join a path on the right (opposite the Horton pub). This path will take you to the village of Bishops Cannings, culminating in two metal gates. Once through the second gate the Crown Inn is directly in front of you with the great spire of the church looming behind.

Expect a warm welcome at the Crown Inn. It is a Waddies pub so you will find a familiar selection of ales. A feature flagged up are the light lunches which are available on Tuesdays and Thursdays; expect dishes like beef chilli, spinach and mushroom tart, and what the landlords call 'Posh Ploughmans'. If you are a largish party you might want to telephone ahead (01380 860218). Lunch service stops at 2.

The Crown Inn, Bishops Cannings

Until the 19th century the people of Chittoe (a hamlet to the north-west) were accustomed to celebrate marriages and bury their dead in Bishops Cannings. Over time this old track across the downs acquired the name of 'The Burying Road'.

4 On leaving the pub turn right and go up the street. At a road intersection go left and walk down to a road junction. Cross over (taking care) and negotiate a metal gate to reach a track that is going away from the road at an angle. This track has a history.

The track climbs gradually, passing through a narrow wooded section before reaching another main road. Turn left and walk for a short distance along the road towards Hill Barn Cottages. Once through them the scenery opens up quite dramatically. Soon to run across you is the old London to Bath road. It is not hard to imagine a coach lurching and rattling across the landscape.

Badly rutted roads meant that coaches often became stuck in the mud or overturned. Axles and wheels broke, horses became lame, luggage fell off and the jolting was so rough that occupants were sometimes thrown out. And there was the constant threat of highway robbery (The Great Road to Bath by Daphne Phillips; Countryside Books, 1983).

(5) And here is the Great Road, not looking so great – did it ever? Turn left and at the main road carry on until arriving at a crossing of tracks. Continue forward passing Hill Cottage (009656) and where a little track comes in from the right turn left and head due south, leaving the Great Road behind you. Quite soon you will notice a car park over to your right. You are on Roundway Hill, scene of a Civil War battle in 1643 or, if you were a Royalist, Runaway Hill on account of the Roundheads fleeing at the sight of Royalist cavalry.

Devizes White Horse in the distance

(6) The last leg of the walk offers fine views of Devizes down below. Cross a minor road before joining another that is adjacent to Roundway Farm. After a very short distance on the road take a track off to the right which will bring you once again to Quakers' Walk. If you look back over to the left you will see a white horse but this time a very modern beast constructed in 1999 in time for the millennium

4 Clyffe Pypard and Bincknoll Castle

Here is a walk that takes in a more than usually life-like white horse, the rather grand site of a Norman castle, a satisfying pub, a church with a cautionary tale to tell and, finally, one of the most picturesque villages in North Wiltshire.

After viewing the white horse there follows a gradual climb up to the escarpment, to what was once a Norman hillfort – Bincknoll Castle (pronounced 'Bynol'). The route then crosses open space to arrive at the large village of Broad Hinton and the Crown Inn. From the pub the route descends to the escarpment before climbing back again and then down again to a village with the wonderful name of

Clyffe Pypard, in whose churchyard are buried a famous person and his wife. The walk concludes

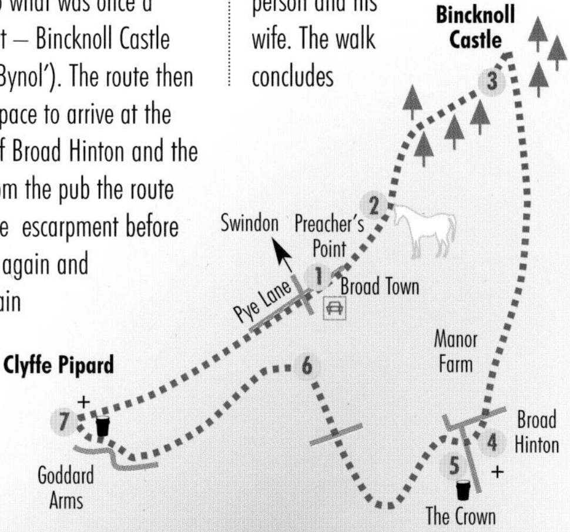

Level: 🥾 🥾
Length: 8 miles (including the church visit)
Terrain: A slow climb at the outset, then largely flat, followed in quick succession by a descent and an ascent, with quite a steep descent towards the end.
Park and Start: In the village of Broad Town south of Swindon at a spot called Preacher's Point (GR 094777). Take care not to obstruct local traffic.
Map: OS Explorer 157
Website: www.goddard-arms.co.uk

by returning via Pye Lane to Broad Town and the evocative Preacher's Point.

(Map labels: Bincknoll Castle, 3, 2, Swindon, Preacher's Point, 1, Pye Lane, Broad Town, Clyffe Pipard, 7, Goddard Arms, 6, Manor Farm, Broad Hinton, 4, 5, The Crown)

1 At Preacher's Point five tracks meet. Pious folks from all points of the compass must have gathered there on Sunday mornings. With the white horse in your sights skirt a bungalow to the left and follow an obvious track to Littletown Farmhouse which is situated directly below the horse.

Morris Marples in his definitive book on white horses, White Horses and other Hill Figures notes, with some approval, that the proportions of this horse are more like those of a natural horse than the majority of other Wiltshire white horses. One local offered a more down to earth view; "Could do with a bit of titivating but the head is there all right; you just can't quite see the top from here."

The Broad Town White Horse

Bincknoll Castle looking North.

2 Go through the gate on the left of the cottage, then through the next gate on the left, marked with a yellow arrow. Proceed along a grass path at the foot of the escarpment. At a junction beneath overhanging trees, go through the gate ahead. Carry on across successive fields, keeping the escarpment on your right.

3 Once through the gate in the hedgerow turn sharp right to climb a wide track that leads to the remains of an ancient hill fort. This is Bincknoll Castle, pronounced 'Bynol', the original Iron Age earthworks having been reinforced by a Norman motte and bailey. Cross the centre of the hillfort to a gate with an arrow pointing straight on along the field

edge. Continue alongside trees on a wide track until a track peels off to the right. Follow it to a farm road and continue until you emerge into Broad Hinton where the Crown Inn can be found opposite the road junction.

The Crown, Broad Hinton

There is a comfortable feel to the Crown Inn – old wood tables, shelves filled with books and intriguing pictures on the walls. Among starters you might find scrambled egg with chorizo, scrambled egg with smoked salmon, black pudding salad, chicken Caesar salad, scallop salad, and devilled whitebait. The beer is from Arkells. The pub is closed all day Monday, and Tuesday lunchtime (01793 731302).

4 After the pub you might want to look in on the church of St Peter ad Vincula which has a wry, even amusing tale to tell of tables

Handless Sir Thomas Wroughton

turned, or hands trumped. To pay a visit pick up a track at the back of the pub and follow it round to the left until the church is visible on the left.

5 If you have been to the church return the way you came but only to the spot where you swung round to reach the church (GR 104763). Turn left (or right if you haven't visited the church) and go through a dogleg before reaching a

byway (Vize Lane). Cross over and continue until you reach a minor road. Again cross over and head for the

The story of the handless man is told by Michael Watson in his book Curiosities of Wiltshire (p.70). It is said that Sir Thomas Wroughton returned from an exhausting hunt to find his wife reading the Bible and no dinner ready. He threw the Bible on the fire but in retrieving it his wife burnt her hands. Thereafter Sir Thomas's hands withered away. St Peter ad Vincula (St Peter in Chains) is the name of a landmark church in Rome.

escarpment. When you reach a track that runs across you turn left.

6 Proceed along the escarpment for 400 yards or so until the path leaves the escarpment by diverging to the left (at Round Wood). Carry on and join the road you crossed before. Walk along the road for a short distance before turning right to descend to the village of Clyffe Pypard. About half-way down look for a path off to the right that will take you straight to the Goddard Arms. After enduring a difficult time it now trades as tea rooms and a bar so, depending on time and taste, you may choose to drop in (check website).

Cliffe is perhaps the most picturesquely seated (sic) village in North Wilts. That was the opinion of the antiquarian A G Bradley in his 1907 book Round and About Wiltshire. *No reason to quarrel with that opinion.*

The side of Clyffe Pypard Church

7 Just beyond the pub car park take a little lane on the right that leads immediately to St Peter's.

Walk through the churchyard to exit through a gate in the far right hand corner. Follow the footpath through several fields to emerge at a road junction beside a house. Continue straight ahead along Pye Lane. The white horse is again visible. The lane emerges at the same crossroads in Broad Town you were at earlier. Cross over into Chapel Lane to reach your car.

Cottage in Clyffe Pypard

Pevsner grave
Clyffe Pypard
Church

In the churchyard, apart from plenty of Goddards, is the grave of the architectural historian and writer, Sir Nikolaus Pevsner, and his wife Lola. The ironwork entrance gates were installed in their memory. A refugee from Hitler's Germany, Pevsner was best known for his 46-volume series of county guides The Buildings of England.

5 The Lydiards and Purton

So many Lydiards, too many to visit. No matter when there is a wild flower paradise to be explored (in season), an Iron Age camp that the Romans annexed, Purton's most famous son to ponder and the top Lydiard venue, Lydiard House, to be admired.

Starting in the high ground west of Purton the first stop is Brockhurst Meadow followed closely by Ringsbury Camp. At a handsome parish church a certain dead Astronomer Royal with a questionable reputation (but adored locally) is conjured up. A look at the Milk House, built in 1656, follows before arriving at the Sun Inn at Lydiard Millicent.

Level: 🏵
Length: 7¾ miles
Terrain: Just the one climb otherwise the going is easy.
Park and Start: Greenhill Village, west of Purton; park on the verge near the telephone box (GR 068862).
Map: OS Explorer 169

After refreshment the route heads for Lydiard House, with its wonderful park setting, before returning to the start.

Map labels

Purton

Ringsbury Camp

3

Restrop

Greenhill

1

8

Hook

4

5 The Milk House

Lydiard Millicent

The Sun Inn 6

7 Lydiard Park

Ringsbury Camp

1 Leaving Greenhill in the direction you came, cross the road and take a track that heads downhill towards a gap in the hedge. Take care as you go because the sods underfoot are liable to be uneven. Head for another gap in the hedge, this one with a gate in it. Now negotiate two more gates before bearing right past a marker. Then it is over a footbridge and through another gate. Watch out for a stile and gate to your right and beyond them a display board. You are entering Brockhurst Meadow.

2 Brockhurst Meadow is quite something in season (above all June) being host to common and spotted orchids, along with a profusion of other wild flowers and grasses.

At the top of the meadow go through a gate and then immediately left up a bank before turning right to enter a field. At the end of the field take a path off to the left. On reaching a junction veer left. Notice to your right a yellow sign saying 'permissive path'. You will need to take this path. Just before some farm gates turn left to reach the Camp.

Ringsbury Camp is an Iron Age hillfort dating from around 50 BC which the Romans took over. Technically, with its double-banked structure, it is a multivallate fort and is unusual for being sited in meadowland.

3 Take the permissive path until it emerges by a house. Across the main road take a path signposted to the church. Proceed across fields through a succession of kissing gates. At a road cross over and go left and then right into Church End where the church is in front of you.

4 St Mary's Purton is a particularly handsome church. Inside, in the south transept, is a

Purton Church

tablet commemorating Nevil Maskelyne, once Astronomer Royal, who died in 1811.

The Maskelyne family had a presence in Purton for over 400 years (the name is derived from 'masculine'). This particular Maskelyne – the most famous of the tribe – is the one Thomas Pynchon had such fun with in his absorbing novel Mason & Dixon. *Dava Sobel pulled no punches either in her book* Longitude. *But here's a thing. In 2011, on the bi-centenary of his death, Purton Historical Society hailed Nevil as Purton's local hero.*

The Milk House

Thomas Gleede inscription

Turn left out of the church and join a road. Go left and follow the road as it curves right. Beyond Purton House there is a sign for the Milk House.

The Milk House or Milkhouse was built in 1656 as the Farm House but by the 18th century seems to have been a dairy. Look for the original owner's name Thomas Gleede carved into a stone at the side you are passing.

5 Just before a gate that leads to the cricket club, cross a footbridge and immediately turn right and walk parallel to the stream until the path converges on and then joins a road – Stone Lane. Go right and follow the road for a short way into the centre of Lydiard Millicent. Turn left to find the Sun Inn about a hundred yards down on the right.

The Sun is an old establishment offering good wholesome food. On the lunch menu you may find grilled salmon with salad and new potatoes, roasted vegetable tartlet topped with glazed parmesan, and Cajun chicken fillet with dressed salad. Expect four ales on tap. There is an agreeable outside terrace for drinking and dining. For opening hours phone 01793 770886.

The Sun Inn, Lydiard Millicent

6 On leaving the pub turn right and walk down the road to a roundabout. Cross the road staying on the same side and almost immediately take a path to the right past some houses. At the end there is a very clear sign to Lydiard House and Park. Cross a bridge cum stile before heading right across the field to an obvious gate. In front of you are cream-coloured and rather swish paths. The house and park are off to the left.

Lydiard House was once the residence of the Bolingbrokes but by 1943 it was empty. Luckily, Swindon Corporation stepped in, bought the property and had it restored. Opened to the public in 1955, the house is open all year round. It is a terrific community asset.

7 Retrace your steps back to the junction where you turned left. Now you need to choose the West Park circuit. When the circuit bears off to the right, get round the first gate by using two other gates. Now look for a stile on the left. Cross it, then follow the fence line of the track down past a rusty gate until another stile comes up on the right. Climb back over to regain the original direction of the track, pass a house to the left and reach a road. Turn right and follow the road on a grassy pavement to reach Hook Farm. Leave the farmyard at the far left. At a gap in the hedge ahead cross a stile after which go left round the edge of the field to reach another stile and beyond a further stile before joining a road.

Lydiard House

8 Up the road is a road signposted to Flaxlands. After 400 yards or so take a path to the right. At the corner of the field do not go left, instead veer right passing the mast which is to your right. From there it is straight into Greenhill.

6 Pewsey and the Kennet & Avon Canal

This walk has everything – water, hills, superb views, a white horse, memories of King Alfred, and even a nature trail within Pewsey itself.

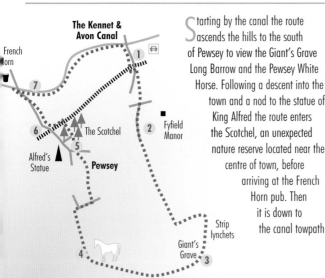

The Kennet & Avon Canal

French Horn

The Scotchel

Fyfield Manor

Alfred's Statue

Pewsey

Strip lynchets

Giant's Grave

Starting by the canal the route ascends the hills to the south of Pewsey to view the Giant's Grave Long Barrow and the Pewsey White Horse. Following a descent into the town and a nod to the statue of King Alfred the route enters the Scotchel, an unexpected nature reserve located near the centre of town, before arriving at the French Horn pub. Then it is down to the canal towpath

Level: 🐾 🐾
Length: 8¾ miles
Terrain: The one climb is near the beginning; otherwise the going is benign with a final section by the canal.
Park and Start: Turn off the Pewsey-Burbage road, the B3087, at a signpost marked 'Milkhouse Water'. After crossing the railway, park on the grass verge just before the canal bridge (GR 175617).
Maps: OS Explorers 130 and 157

and a pleasant saunter back to the car.

1 Walk away from the canal back down the road you came along. After crossing the railway bridge look out for a footpath to the left opposite a drive. Before long a path appears running across you. Turn right and continue to the Pewsey-Burbage road. Cross over to Fyfield,

> *Fyfield Manor (not open) has parts which date back to the 15th century. In the 1960s it was the home of Sir Anthony Eden. Touted for years as Churchill's successor his career suffered a calamitous setback when he invaded Egypt following Nasser's seizure of the Suez Canal.*

not so much a hamlet as the manor — on the left — and a few other houses.

2 Carry on down the road until you are obliged to continue on a grassy track. Ahead can be seen an extensive ancient field system — strip lynchets — stretching across the hills. Once past a wind pump the track dictates you turn left and climb up the side of the escarpment. At the top bear right and then right again. You are on Fyfield Down.

3 Now heading west, look out for a feature to the right that is obviously a barrow. In fact it is the Giant's Grave Long Barrow. Follow the contour of the hill round, past a clump of trees. You are on Pewsey Hill with marvellous views over the Vale of

View to Giant's grave

Pewsey. Since this is open access land you are at liberty to pick out your own path. Sticking to the contour, and keeping a fence to your left, you will

Pewsey White Horse

It is not the first white horse on the site; the first was cut around 1785. But by the 1930s the chalk was no longer visible (which happens to white horses). A man called George Marples (father of Morris, see the Clyffe Pypard walk) was researching the old Pewsey horse when he was approached to design a new horse. The new horse was cut in the last weeks of April 1937.

soon the side of an enclosure. Inside that enclosure, situated at around 500 feet above sea level, is to be found the Pewsey White Horse.

Looking down on the Vale of Pewsey

4 The descent is along the Green Drove. At the bottom turn right and walk along the road to Green Drove Farm. Take the signed footpath on the left and continue across open ground to a road. Carry on along a metalled path until another road is reached. Pass some country cottages that might have come out of *Lark Rise to Candleford*; this really is a very pleasant quarter of Pewsey. Now cross a bridge and head slightly uphill until a three-way junction is reached. At the recreation ground turn left and then right, keeping the football pitch to your right. A gap to the left comes up. Take it and skirt some tennis courts. Veer left and drop down keeping the store to your left. At the store front turn right and very soon you are in Pewsey High Street. Impossible to miss is the statue to King Alfred, crowned King of Wessex in 870 and owner of much of the land in the Pewsey Vale.

5 Cross the road and follow the pavement round to the right. A little way on, to the right, is Broomcroft Road. About 150 yards along on the left is the entrance to a nature reserve, the Scotchel. Go through a gate into the reserve and join the King Alfred Trail. The path winds alongside a stream – the infant River Avon. How wonderful to find such a trail in the middle of a town! After leaving the reserve carry on up the path to arrive at a minor road by a railway arch. Go right through the arch and immediately left onto a firmly surfaced path. Carry on past

rows of vines to your left until you reach a main road.

6 Go right along the road (there is a pavement) for 700 yards or so until a bridge over the canal

The French Horn is a cosy and welcoming establishment. For lunch the staple is liable to be a filled ciabatta served with fresh salad and chips. On offer might be bacon and brie, sausage and onion, and cheese and tomato melt. Also on the menu expect items such as crispy beer-battered fish and chips with peas. Being a Waddies pub, expect 6X, Henry's IPA and one other. Lunch opening times are 12-3 except for Tuesday when the place is closed; telephone 01672 562443

comes into view. On the other side of the bridge and to the left is the French Horn pub. Ahead of you over to the north-east is another and rather larger Giant's Grave Long Barrow.

7 After leaving the pub there is more water and hill scenery to enjoy. Cross the bridge and drop down to the canal towpath before proceeding eastwards. Pass under Pains Bridge and at the next bridge leave the canal to find the car.

The French Horn

7 Wansdyke and West Woods

This walk offers a feast of sarsens, some ridge walking with especially attractive views, a deserted medieval village but with hardly a thing to see, and a visit to a large area of woods beloved of bluebell enthusiasts. All in just over 5 miles.

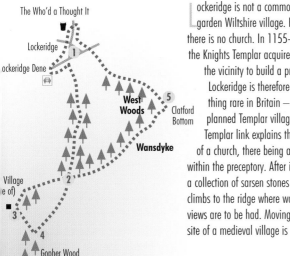

The Who'd a Thought It

Lockeridge

Lockeridge Dene

West Woods

Clatford Bottom

5

Wansdyke

Village (site of)

Gopher Wood

Lockeridge is not a common or garden Wiltshire village. For a start there is no church. In 1155-56 the Knights Templar acquired land in the vicinity to build a preceptory. Lockeridge is therefore something rare in Britain – a planned Templar village. The Templar link explains the absence of a church, there being a church within the preceptory. After inspecting a collection of sarsen stones the route climbs to the ridge where wonderful views are to be had. Moving west the site of a medieval village is

Level:

Length: 5½ miles

Terrain: There is a haul up at the start with a lesser shorter climb coming later on. Unless walking through woods is a concern there should be no worries.

Park and Start: Lockeridge Dene, just south of the village; park on the curve. The village of Lockeridge is just south of the A4, three miles west of Marlborough. Drive through the village past the pub to the start point (GR 147675).

Map: OS Explorer 157

Website: andrewgough.co.uk/forum/viewtopic.php?f=30&t=3201(about Gopher Wood)

encountered just south of the Wansdyke, itself reckoned to be a

41

linear defensive earthwork dating from the Dark Ages. After touching on a feature called Gopher Wood the route again picks up the Wansdyke Path before entering West Woods, a dense tract of woodland cum forest. West Woods' claim to fame is the visual feast of bluebells in the spring and the effect is spectacular. The walk concludes by travelling the short distance to Lockeridge.

 Lockeridge Dene is a National Trust site and conservation area, perhaps more significant than appears at first glance because of the sarsen stones scattered over the area.

Across the road from the site is a footpath signed to Huish. Commence a gradual and more or less straight

Sarsens are sometimes referred to as 'druid stones' or 'grey wethers', the latter due to their resemblance at a distance to a flock of sheep, the word 'wether' coming from the Old English for sheep. They are scattered all over the Marlborough Downs. Some buildings in the village feature sarsen stone (generally painted or left rough-hewn) thatched with wheat or wheat-reed mix.

climb up to the ridge with a dip as you pass through an open space.

② At the top bear right and once fully in the open follow what

Lockeridge Dene

is the Wansdyke Path admiring the fine views over to the left. You are headed for where a medieval village called Shaw once stood. As a general rule the Wansdyke Path shadows the Wansdyke but a diversion was created from the course of the Wansdyke (which is visible ahead of you) in order to skirt the village site.

Site of Shaw Village

One of the largest linear earthworks in the UK, Wansdyke runs from the Avon valley south of Bristol to just before Savernake Forest. The construction period is thought to be the 5th century. With a deep ditch in front, and running in an east-west alignment, it looks as if the earthwork was built to keep invading Saxons away from the indigenous Romano-British.
As for the name, it may have been dedicated to Woden by pagan Saxons.

By 1066 Shaw was divided between two owners, and so it continued until its demise, which may have occurred in the 15th century. By 1377 it was the smallest economic unit in Wiltshire to be taxed, with only three payers; it is missing from a list of small settlements in 1428 and so by then was probably deserted.

Bluebells in West Woods

Turn left past Shaw Copse and stop to look across at the village although little if anything remains to see (although some say a street may be discerned).

(3) Now carry on in the same direction towards a wooded section. This is Gopher Wood about which much can be learned from the website, notably a fascinating Biblical digression. The route now veers left round the wood to reach its north-east corner (142645). Here ignore the criss-cross of paths coming in from right and left in favour of a track more or less straight ahead that leads to the dark green mass that is West Woods.

(4) On reaching the edge of West Woods you will be at the spot where you docked at the end of the first section. The way ahead now is to the right. You are back on the Wansdyke Path. Continue for a

Gopher Wood

mile or so until the Wansdyke Path turns abruptly to the right (164665). Your path however lies to the left and it takes you past the parking spot used in April and May by bluebell aficionados. This is Clatford Bottom and to call the ground 'carpeted' is no exaggeration.

(5) Leaving the parking place head up through the trees and continue curving left until you emerge from West Woods. Ahead of you is a broad track that soon becomes a road. Follow the road down to a junction. Cross over and at the main road turn right for the Who'd a Thought It.

Turn right when leaving the pub to find your car just round the curve.

The Who'd a Thought It is a Waddies pub so expect 6X and Henry's IPA flanked by a guest ale plus lager, cider, wine and fruit juices. There is a snack menu with sandwiches, baguettes and jacket potatoes with various fillings on offer (e.g. tuna mayo, mozzarella, tomato and basil). Dishes likely to catch the eye are warm salad of chicken livers and Stornoway black pudding; also moules marinière served as a starter or as a main. The pub is closed on Mondays. For more information, phone 01672 861255.

The 'Who'd a Thought It'

8 Aldbourne and Snap

Aldbourne is a large village that has been here for over 1000 years. The only occupation it has known was by American troops in World War 2. Themes on this walk include rabbits, and a deserted village but the views are the thing especially in the first half. Add in the ambience of Aldbourne itself and you have a walk to savour.

Level: 🥾 🥾
Length: 8½ miles
Terrain: There is an ascent at the beginning with a much shorter climb coming later on, a scramble really; all the same a genuine two boots walk.
Park and Start: Aldbourne, by the Green and the Blue Boar pub (GR 265757).
Map: OS Explorer 157

Aldbourne has two pubs and an e-magazine that is lively and informative. Starting by the church the walk proceeds upwards through a knot of barrows to stand above a once-famous rabbit warren that in medieval times supplied a king's table. At the top of what is known as Sugar Hill the route turns west down an old Saxon way called the Thieves' Way. The next section joins up with the Ridgeway which is followed south before a turn back east brings up the deserted medieval village of Snap but with nothing to see. To wrap things up, the walk follows a hill ridge back down to Aldbourne.

Swindon

3 Sugar Hill

4

5

Aldbourne Warren

2

Four Barrows

Snap **6**

Aldbourne Chase

1 **Aldbourne**

Hungerford

The Blue Boar

There has been an inn on the site of the Blue Boar since the 15th century. Being a Waddies house, 6X and IPA are always on tap. Specials are changed regularly. On the day the writer visited (a Tuesday), on offer were: tuna niçoise, pork and red onion sausages, duck breast with ginger, Cajun chicken salad and beef chilli and rice. With the Green adorned by fine old dwellings, the Celtic cross and the 15th century church, eating and drinking outside is a pleasure. To book (recommended at weekends) phone 01672 540237.

1 Go up the road by the church past what is known as Crooked Corner to reach a parting of the ways. Take the track to the left and head uphill. Once on the ridge it is not too long before you arrive at a feature known as the Four Barrows, three of which touch and sit in a line. There is so much evidence of a prehistoric presence on this walk, as on other walks in this book and in Wiltshire generally.

2 Thread a way through the barrows and press on. Before long, if you cast your gaze over to the left, you will spot Aldbourne Warren Farm.

Aldbourne Green

There was a time when Aldbourne Warren was celebrated as producing 'the best, sweetest and fattest rabbits in England'. The king himself, Henry IV, had Aldbourne conies sent to London for his table. How long did that take and what condition were the rabbits in when they arrived? It was estimated that in 1720 there were 24,000 rabbits in the farmed warrens of the area! Rabbit-warrening ended when the land was ploughed during the Napoleonic Wars to grow wheat.

Carry on along the track keeping the field boundary to your right until you reach the top of what is called Sugar Hill.

(3) With a wooded section to your right turn left and at a junction of paths carry on in the same direction following the track down to the road. Along the way there is a chance to appreciate Aldbourne Warren to the left and Lidlington Warren to the right. Perfectly west-facing, they put north-facing Watership Down in the shade.

The track you are on is known as the Thieves' Way, in all likelihood a drove for stolen cattle.

Snap ahead

Looking over Snap

A view back to Sugar Hill

(4) Cross the road and go down a slight dip before it becomes necessary to bear left and make a short pull up an incline. Once at the top you are on the Ridgeway.

(5) Head south on the Ridgeway for half a mile, at one point crossing a track running across you. At the next left leave the Ridgeway and aim for a gate at the far side of a bumpy field. Once through the gate go down the track to the site of what was once Snap village (or Snape).

You would need *Time Team* to spot anything significant. A plunge into the undergrowth would be adventurous but don't do it.

(6) Follow the hedge line to a point where over to the left is the cluster of properties that is Upper Upham (Upham was another deserted village situated behind the Eliza-bethan manor house). Do not head up there but instead pass another path to Upper Upham and carry on in the direction of Aldbourne. You are

entering Aldbourne Chase and some-where along here there was a Civil War skirmish on 18th September 1643 when Prince Rupert and his Cavaliers tangled inconclusively with the Parliamentary Army, two days before the real encounter that was the First Battle of Newbury. Now the route drops down the hill ridge until it again meets the Aldbourne - Swindon road. Turn right and walk back to the car taking care on what is a busy road. At the village centre turn left to pass the other pub, the Crown, stand-ing more or less opposite the village pond. Depending on the opening hours of this establishment and those of the Blue Boar, and how thirsty you are and how much you want to get home, you might end up tossing a coin to decide which hostelry to visit.

Snap was always small. Apart from the Civil War skirmish close by, nothing ever really happened. The beginning of the end came in 1905 when an entrepreneurial butcher bought Snap and the surrounding land. The population was reduced to two elderly people by 1909 and finally the one remaining villager was persuaded to move to Aldbourne. By 1914 Snap was deserted.

9 Savernake Forest, Great Bedwyn and Wilton

Forest and water, Roman occupation, and early industrial machinery emerge as themes on this walk.

Starting at the hamlet of St. Katharine's on the edge of Savernake Forest, the route docks first at Chisbury with its Roman connections before dropping down to Great Bedwyn on the Kennet & Avon canal. Above Great Bedwyn was once a Romano-British villa and the walk passes through the site en route to an iconic landmark – Wilton Windmill. Down below in the village of Wilton is the excellent Swan Inn. The walk then returns to the canal and takes in Crofton Pumping Station and the Crofton Beam Engines before crossing

Level: 🥾 🥾
Length: 8½ miles
Terrain: The longest climb comes in the middle with the route from the canal up to the windmill. There is a level crossing to be negotiated so the usual care will need to be taken.
Park and Start: St Katherine's, at the T-junction where the road past the church peters out (GR 976772).
Map: OS Explorer 157
Websites: www.wiltonwindmill.co.uk
www.croftonbeamengines.org

a railway and completing the walk along farmland and woodland tracks.

1 Set off east along the track signposted Chisbury and Stokke. It is hard to imagine a more magical place to start a walk than the remote spot you have just left. A church, a church school and a sprin-

> St Katherine's church, completed in 1861, is definitive Victorian Gothic - with knobs on. The carriage drive up to the porch door was clearly intended for the aristocracy. Cue Maria Caroline, Marchioness of Ailesbury, who dedicated the church in memory of her Russian mother; Katharine Woronzoff, Dowager Countess of Pembroke.

St Katherine's church

kling of properties: that is the extent of St Katherine's.

Continue along the track. At the junction where the signpost says 'Stokke',

turn left past some houses and follow the semi-metalled lane up to a road.

2 Cross over and continue along a lane. At a road junction take the left fork. Very soon a gate comes up on the right. Go up the field to another gate and beyond that a third gate should the farm gate not be open. At the far right-hand corner of the field, level with a telegraph pole, turn right and cross the field in front of you without altering direction, before bearing slightly right to enter the next field. At the top look out for a stile over to the left. Cross it and then another before shooting down a narrow path over to the left to reach Chisbury Green.

3 Chisbury is a pleasant spot worth a pause. Take the Great Bedwyn road but only for a few yards until a stile appears to the right. Cross the field and go over another stile. Inside the fenced enclosure to your left was once an Iron Age hillfort. Head over to the wooded section on the right and enter the woods for a couple of hundred yards before exiting. Of the two tracks take the one to the left and cross the field to reach a road.

4 The road leads to Great Bedwyn. At the road junction turn left. Carry on down to reach the Kennet & Avon Canal bridge. Once over the bridge turn right to join the towpath. Here you are with the boaters. Expect a busy scene, especially at weekends. Ahead is a lock with an old bridge over it. Go left through a gate and leave the canal.

5 Climb the grassy slope and follow a winding path into the woods for half a mile or so until you reach a point where farm tracks come in from left and right. This is Castle Copse where in the late 18th century a Romano-British villa complex was discovered.

The most recent excavators of Castle Copse (1983-86) concluded that the site may have evolved from a settlement in or around Chisbury hillfort to become a large stone-built courtyard villa in the 3rd and 4th centuries, before abandonment.

Carry on through what is known as the Brail until a sign to the right signals Wilton Windmill. Bear round

Savernake Forest, Great Bedwyn and Wilton

Wilton Windmill

After the completion of the Kennet & Avon Canal a source of power was needed to replace the watermills made redundant by the loss of their water source to the canal, thus the construction of the windmill in 1821. It is the only working windmill in Wiltshire.

At the Swan Inn service is pleasant, friendly and helpful. Meat is sourced locally and everything is home-cooked. A specials board changes every day. Dishes you might expect to see are grilled sardines, mussels cooked in cider, dressed crab, braised pig cheek, and roast guinea fowl. Otherwise there are sandwiches and baguettes. Ramsbury Ale is brewed nearby. In fine weather eating outside is a definite option. The number is 01672 870274.

to the left and at a T-junction of tracks go left to reach a road. There to the right is the windmill.

(6) If the windmill is open you may choose to visit it; whatever you decide to do continue down to Wilton village where the Swan Inn awaits.

On leaving the pub turn left down the road past a duck pond. The path you want is over to the right, not straight ahead up the field but to the left. Skirt the field edge and very soon you will become aware of a stretch of water to your left. This is Wilton Water. Follow it down to the canal.

At the canal there is a new iconic sight to take in — the tall chimney of Crofton Pumping Station. Turn right

Savernake Forest, Great Bedwyn and Wilton

Wilton Water (or Wide Waters) was created in the early 19th century by damming a narrow valley. It is fed by natural springs and in addition to providing water for the canal provides a haven for wildlife.

Crofton Pumping Station with the 'Even More Therapeutic'.

and follow the towpath along to a bridge. There exit through a gate and go left over the bridge. In front of you is the London-Exeter line. Taking great care, cross over to Crofton.

(7) Go down the road and at the first junction turn left. At the top of a rise go right up a dead-end road past Crofton Manor Farm. When the road runs out, turn right keeping to the field edge. At the top go

slightly right and then left into a wooded section. Before long there is open land and a large house to the right. Turn left at the next house to join a track that soon becomes a

Perhaps better known than the pumping station are the Crofton Beam Engines that pump the water in the canal. The engines are only "in steam" at certain times (check the website).

semi-metalled lane. Pass by an open area — Stokke Common — and keep bearing right to arrive at a three-way junction in front of a house, Stokke Manor.

(8) Just down the track is the junction you met at the start of the walk. Carry on to St Katherine's. It is a pleasant end to the outing.

10 Wexcombe, Chute Causeway and Hippenscombe

The Romans were no quitters but an instance happened here. This walk has so many winning elements to it, not least a great pub in the middle.

Level: 🥾 🥾 (🥾)
Length: 9 miles
Terrain: An ascent to start with followed by a descent. Later there is a steep descent followed by quite a steep but short ascent and then another of the same description but even shorter. Definitely a two boots walk perhaps a three.
Park and Start: Wexcombe; drive through the village and bear left at a T-junction sign. Park at the end of the cul-de-sac taking care not to block anyone's access or exit (GR 273588).
Map: OS Explorer 131

The scenery on this walk in the far north-east of the county is quite dazzling. Starting in the hamlet of Wexcombe the route heads south past a former inn with dubious associations before reaching a pub with a fine and growing reputation and glorious views to boot. Turning north a most unusual feature is encountered — Hippenscombe, the valley that the Romans, en route from Winchester to Cirencester, chose to avoid. Thus thwarted, the Romans were obliged to introduce a deviation from the straight, a kink which came to be known as Chute Causeway. After crossing the Causeway the route descends into Hippenscombe valley bottom and then up to the northern ridge where there are superb views to north and south and back to the east. It remains to reach single-street Tidcombe before returning to the start.

1 Follow the track up the hill. Over and behind to the right a small brown building with a round pineapple-style roof catches the eye. What can it be? Take a moment to turn round and enjoy a marvellous birds-eye view of Wexcombe. Over in the middle distance with its

unmistakeable white blades is the exquisite Wilton Windmill.

The small brown building was once a working pump house. Erected in 1899 it bears a plaque 'Wexcombe Water Works' but is now classified as a folly. Wilton Windmill, as the only working windmill in the South-West, is far from being a folly.

The downhill stretch that follows is exhilarating, passing first a long barrow to the right and a trig point and reservoir to the left. At the bottom of the track go through a small gate to enter a field. An isolated cottage can be seen ahead and to the left a road. Head straight for the building

Wexcombe and Wilton Windmill

Quince Cottage

In the early 19th century Scot's Poor was an alehouse called the Blue Bell Inn frequented by the drovers who used these downland tracks. It was closed abruptly in August 1914. A local farmer encountered by the writer said the place was renowned as a poachers' hang-out and that perhaps was the reason for its closure – or maybe it was the onset of war.

which is called Scot's Poor and sits at a three-way junction where the Roman road crossed prehistoric trails.

2 Once on the road – the impressive Chute Causeway – turn left and stay on the left. After 50 yards or so, peer over the side. There below is Hippenscombe. It is a startling sight. No place for a road though. The Romans were no quitters but they were wise to go for the kink. Carry on along the Causeway

for a short distance until a broad track comes up on the right. At a T-junction go left and climb a hill admiring as you go a beautiful

farmhouse to the left. This is the western edge of Upper Chute village and at the top of the hill is the Cross Keys Inn.

Dean Farm

The Cross Keys

*At the Cross Keys Inn expect
the daily bar menu to include
home-made soups, pork
and leek sausage and mash
with onion gravy, and beer-
battered cod and chips.
Pies are a speciality with the
star item being a game pie.
Expect to see three beers on
tap – a regular (Fuller's
London Pride), a guest beer,
and a beer sourced from
within 30 miles of the pub.
To check opening hours
and serving times call
01264 730295.*

3 On leaving the pub turn left towards the village and take the first side road to the left up to the church – St Nicholas of Chute and Chute Forest. Just past the church on the right is a gate. Once into the field look for another gate diagonally opposite after which turn right to join a road. Continue until a 'Private' board makes it necessary to turn left and head up Breach Lane until arriving once again at Chute Causeway. Hippenscombe is next. Cross over the road and proceed downhill to reach the valley bottom.

4 Still heading north wind your way through the collection of buildings that is Hippenscombe, passing to the right of a long grey barn. Over to the left is a wildly undulating feature called The Slay. Once the ridge is reached pause to take in where you have come from; then go left and carry on westwards. This is a particularly enjoyable stretch. When Chute Causeway comes up again cross over and take the track down to Tidcombe, passing first a long barrow to the left and then skirting a small copse to arrive at a stile at the far end of the field. Once in the

The Slay above Hippenscombe

Looking back east on the northern ridge above Hippenscombe

Wexcombe, Chute Causeway and Hippenscombe

Looking north from the ridge

valley bottom look up for a stile in front of the house above you. After negotiating the stile turn right into single-street Tidcombe.

5 Befitting its remote upland position the church is dedicated to St Michael, the winged messenger of the air. Go through the church gate and cross the graveyard admiring as you go the fine Manor House to the right. Leaving the grave-yard behind cross over the track that leads down to the Manor House before bearing immediately left to follow a fence. At the end ignore the track off to the left and, following a white stick in the ground and a

marker on a tree, continue to a field at the bottom where the houses of Wexcombe are visible over to the left. Follow the edge of the field until a field corner is reached at which point turn right. Carry on along the track, at the first field boundary going right and then left before proceeding straight ahead. The start is so clearly visible over to the left that you will see the track you need to take to get there. On gaining the track turn left and walk the 150 yards or so back to the car.

Manor House, Tidcombe